Endless I Will Be

Sonia Oinam

INDIA • SINGAPORE • MALAYSIA

ISBN 979-8-89186-556-3

Dedication

To my beloved parents (L) Oinam Daoji and (L) Oinam *Ongbi* Memcha. Even if you have left for the heavenly abode, you will reside in my heart forever.

To my life-partner Yaiphaba Longjam, my heart beats Machanghen Longjam and Yailen Longjam.

Contents

SECTION – III
HOPE

Winged Words

For the last two years, I have been haunted by the literal meaning of some lines:

'Poetry makes nothing happen...'

– W.H. Auden

'A poem cannot stop a bullet. A novel can't defuse a bomb...'

– Salman Rushdie

'In one sense, the efficacy of poetry is nil-no lyric has ever stopped a tank...'

– Seamus Heaney

Disturbed, I have been. Yes, I have been deeply disturbed day in and day out. And I hear myself asking: What is poetry? And what is its relevance in the hard times we live in? Perhaps, it is because of this disturbance that I decided to deliver the 7th Kabi Chaoba Memorial Lecture on the self-chosen topic - the Relevance of Poetry in the Modern Age. Satisfied? Far from it. Poetry and its relevance today are a big question to me. And I would like to ask the question to its bitter end. Come rains, come shine. The answer to the question is synonymous with my quest for identity and the meaning of life - who am I? What is my place in the cosmos? My tryst with the question finds expression in my prefaces of two collections of poems (Manipuri) published last year and another this year. Altogether, the prefaces cover some 100 pages in small print on demy size paper. The question is still alive and kicking.

The woods are lovely, dark and deep,
But I have promises to keep,
And miles to go before I sleep,
And miles to go before I sleep.

– Robert Frost

At this juncture, Sonia came with her manuscript of poems in English. I emphasise 'English' because English is not the first language of Sonia. I was taken by surprise - I had no inkling of her interest and inclination in literature. She is an officer of the State Civil Service of Manipur, and she was then working as Under Secretary of one of the Departments under my charge. I retired on reaching the age of superannuation on 28.2.2018. And she came to me at the far end of 2022. She left her manuscript. I read; frankly, I tried to read. Here is someone who finds music in the old form of words and the spoken form of a language as well. Hers is a marriage of the two. I returned her manuscript with some comments. But that was not the end of the story. After some weeks, she came back. This is a new Sonia, and her writing shows a marked difference. I do not know if I have met a poet, or poetess to be precise, in the making. I have to accept it as it is, and I try to convince myself that here is one soul who seems to be convinced of the relevance of poetry in the modern days and perhaps, in the days to come. When she returned with her manuscript, retouched all over again, I said, 'go ahead', Bless!

Imphal, **K. Radhakumar Singh, IAS(Retd.)**
16.03.2023

Acknowledgement

I extend my gratitude to Shri Radhakumar Kangjam, Retired IAS, for taking out his precious time to read my poems and also for his views and suggestions on the poems, and for his words of encouragement in bringing out this poetry book.

I am thankful to Shri Pradip Phanjoubam, Senior journalist and author, for agreeing to review my poems even before the book was published. I am thankful to him for his precious time and earnest review.

I am also thankful to Shri Beeshantam Yumnam for his beautiful illustrations for the poetry book and also for all the help and guidance in bringing out this publication.

I am thankful to my elder sister Dr. Promila Oinam, sister-in-law Inoulembi Longjam, and all my dear friends who were always eager to read my poems, and am thankful for their feedback.

I am grateful to my husband Yaiphaba Longjam who encouraged me to publish my collection of poems and supported me in all my endeavours.

Last but not least, I am grateful to the entire team of Notion Press for the wonderful work in bringing out this publication.

– Sonia Oinam

SECTION – I

BEHOLD NOT

Uneasy Heart

It is sheer folly of man,
unguarded, the heart it keeps.
Only that it suffers
when it starts to beat.

The heart beats to break,
simple is the end, already known.
Why is it unaware?
Or is it a daring joy!

Smile, smile as ever you wish,
say not a word, young lovey.
Gazes in admiration have opened this entangled road,
with a gift of hurt and pain.

And still, you beat,
and still, you hurt,
and still, you part,
and still, you burn the passion.

A long way to wait,
to solve the riddle.

Hardly One Understands

Hardly one understands why
one singles out another from a crowd
that touches one's soul.

Hardly one understands why
one resents one's desire,
pretends and hides not to be seen.

Hardly one understands why
one's heart pounds so hard
that one fears it would be heard.

Hardly one understands why
one has so much to say
that one falls short of words.

Hardly one understands why
one's coyness cleaves it all
and leaves another to stare in vain.

Hardly one understands why
one binds one's heart in chains
that guards it in utmost care.

Hardly one understands
one's own restraints
then leads to one's own loneliness.

In the Mist

This wintry solitude
has shrouded you in the mist,
and a burning desire I have
to see you as the mist clears.

I live merrily,
singing and smiling and laughing,
a glimpse of you in the mist
wakes me up to find you nowhere.

I can hardly move in this wintry cold,
but I shall not give up the path I faintly see
in the mist
that will lead me to you.

Autumn

Inevitable is joy and happiness,
sorrow and pain as well;
a month does come,
Oh! Autumn, awful Autumn,
the month of withered leaves
of thought and of body.

The mind is occupied with chaos
when Autumn ye stay.
No one finds joy and peace,
only a pain, the pain of departure;
from thine Beloved ones,
Oh! Dear Father, our guardian,
You leave us here alone,
alone in this world led by the blind
Forever.

Breezes of Hope

Hopes reverberate through
the ground baked by the scorching sun,
as I spend the day
looking at the leaves tossed in the wind.

Few breezing through my hair,
the clouds turn greyer;
Alas! The sky growls,
growls and grumbles all night.

Pouring out droplets from above
and washing away all the dirt.
And as the morning dawns,
ye Earth is all wet and anew.

Calm and glowing with life,
chirping friends sing a new song
as the first rays of the sun send
breezes of hope and love
to you and I.

Joy of Love

The joy of love fills and fills,
and tells us
to treat people with love and tender care.
When a precious heart is offered,
lest they get hurt
and broken.

Take time to yield
to your whims.
Lest you gift them
tears to shed
and in return for their love
Ungratefulness!

The joy of love fills and fills,
and also forgives;
it finds no fault
and no reason it has,
blindfolded you may walk
but Love will find a way out.

Love is God

O Love, powerful love
maketh me live on.
O Venus, trying me through thick and thin!
O Mercury, taking me to duty and justice!
O Poetry, bringing me to peace in the abyss!

O Changes, ye who changes
thy life, mind, and belief;
lost and gone in the end
to ye Love I fall,
to ye I belong!

O Wit, in this journey I learn
Love is God and God is Love.

The Fire Burnt Away

The fire burnt away
and turned to ashes, old memories—
closed eyes falter to arrest melting snow
frozen long ago.

The moon rises to the zenith,
no warmth or gloom
and shines empty,
gloating a day's pleasure.

Glittery stars drift apart,
guiltily, feeling the mockery.
Tired wind hushes a sigh
and falls asleep in the still night.

Belying every moment—
The fire burnt away the blessing.

In Love with You

Death be better in a life without you,
for every heartbeat spring from you;
you are in every breath I take in
and life is music with you in my heart.

The whispering winds
and the rain showers on our love;
I am unafraid of the world now,
for a strength I have found,
let them know
I am in love with you.

My prayers have been answered
of a blessing for us together;
my prayers to Thee
of this love divine—
today, tomorrow until death makes us apart.

Moments That Keep Us Alive

Strange are we to run away,
yes, away from the truth
from which we draw inspiration—
the things, moments, and people.

We remain as a fool
to let a moment pass,
a priceless moment that appeals
and which cannot be bought or stolen.

Each unguarded moment brings us
tremendous happiness in the end;
search, search for these moments
that remains hidden
which fulfills life.

Embrace the moment that comes,
for they are the moments that keep us alive.

Forget Me

Forget me in joy and in merriment
and I wouldn't mind;
Forget me in success and in good fortune
and I wouldn't mind.

Forget me in your bad times
and I would really mind;
remember me
in your tiresome and hard moments.

In sorrow, allow me to share,
I'll suffer all your pangs of sorrow—
my happiness it'll be
grant me this wish.

Remember me
whenever empty you feel;
let my presence fill
The void!

Endless I Will Be

When I shall be gone, I shall be gone,
I will not smile; I will not laugh.
I will not be seen, anywhere,
and only in memoriam, I will remain.

When I shall be gone, I shall be gone,
I will not be angry; I will not be crying.
I will not despair of a true time,
and only a spring will end.

When I shall be gone, I shall be gone,
I will not ask; I will not answer.
I know when I die, I will be gone,
what for is health, wealth and fame?

I live with my heart, with faith over fear,
and bury myself in the words I treasure most.
Endless I will be—
when only my words will remain.

Behold Not

Behold not unfallen tears,
behold not an ocean within;
a wave, falling and rising like a tide
day and night, weeks and months.
leave the tears to fall free,
shed free, glistening on thy cheek;
unburden a heavy load,
and let a smile brighten thy face.
Stronger thou will become
with each steep step thou climb;
with every slow and steady effort made
to chase away differing thoughts.
Gloomy days may come
and will be gone;
Sunny days will come.
behold a hope, a hope to recover.

O! Full Moon

O! Lovely moon, bridal moon,
Why appear so bright to burn?
The unhealed heart,
The wound bleeds afresh.
A long-time unseen, my love,
Then what glee smiles ye so?
O! gathering clouds, hide her
In the deep night;
Like a darkness that surrounds
And paints everything in black.
My only desire is these serene chilly winds,
Away from the full moon's gleam.

Reflecting Rain

While the sky is deep and sullen,
the clouds grow old and dark.
Is it a burst of thine anger?
Is it a burst of thine laughter?
Whirling and tossing tender leaves,
crashing on my poor thatch,
waking me up now and then;
reflecting and taking me back in time!
Ye droplets sprinkled in entirety;
chilling souls in a way
amidst joyous laughs.
Reflecting rain, why ye?
Why ye bring endless hopes?
To run, run thither back to river,
to hide and seep into the earth.
Pray, pray thou'll not leave.
stay, soak me divine drops.

Thy Homecoming

Memories come haunting,
Hopes come dancing.
Oh! fateful, dreadful days,
Would tomorrow be different?
As love grows weeds and reeds,
And as tortoise time goes by.
And life flies high,
Up and in and out.
The soul, freed like a bird,
Await thy homecoming.
To gleefully dance
Round and round and round.

You Make Me Smile

You make me smile,
you make my day.
Your smile adorns contentment,
your spirit high and seeking;
but to my eye,
your pride radiates.
I climb up a rocky ledge,
to find you lying on a barren land;
far on the other side,
arid and vast and unsettling,
I live in full bloom
on the peak of this rocky ledge.
far from the madding crowd,
you come into view and make me smile.

Wish To See You Again

In search of a set of words,
to pluck at my heartstrings;
for someone I know, I do not know,
reasons and reasons, fear and adoration.
A smile to lean upon—
and a few moments,
for once I would like to move
the mountain that separates
You and I.
Casting away this shyness.
O! Unguarded moments,
you are the dearest.
What life would bring next,
I do not know!
But I do know,
tucked in the corner of my heart,
I wish to see you again!

My Love

If, my Love, we never had met,
My days would still be empty;
The days would have passed
With work, with gossip, with friends—
But the nights would still be empty,
Piercing lonely heart,
And the tears would have never dried.
My Love,
Empty days and nights have passed,
And I live in these glorious moments,
With a glorious you!
My Love,
My life is now filled
With peace and love.

As Days Go By

As days go by,
No, a day hasn't gone
Without thy thoughts in my mind.
As days go by,
I know thou reside in my heart and soul,
Missing thy friendly, funny woos.
As days go by,
Dances and drums fade away,
Only lonely heart aches.
As days go by,
The path seems adrift,
As days go by and by.

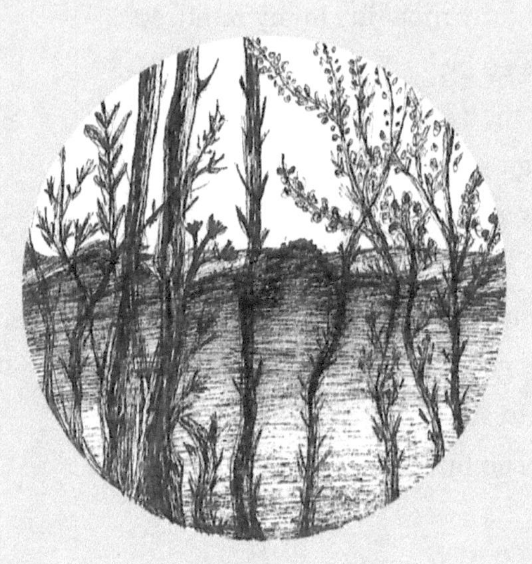

Whisper in the Wind

Listen, listen to the wind,
close thy tired eyes,
feel thy breath and forget all worries;
listen to none of the utterances,
but a whisper in the wind.
Somebody whispers
stealthily—
A confession of care
to thy heart,
to calm and
uncage the controlling mind.
Love struggles to free itself,
from the shackles of mind
and will heal all wounds,
each and every hurt,
for love is not lost;
the undying love.

Tonight, I Remember

Tonight, I remember,
verses and songs in a flash,
tunes unheard of long are played again,
and I dream with my eyes closed;
unceasing thoughts play like an untiring child.
If the earth could stop moving awhile,
I would bid farewell to the past,
all the fears and parting of ways.
Tonight, I remember and rejoice—
a smile is rooted around,
a legacy of a silent gaze, a silent word;
to embrace a fate,
to cherish a moment,
through laughs and cries,
through days and nights,
a tale time will tell.

Fren

Fren, I called you so,
for you, I giggled and laughed,
for you, I dared and tried,
as true friends do.
Fren, I do not hate you,
I do not hate life.
Fren, I do hate my heart,
for not knowing the true you.
Fren, I was your fren,
I wasn't wary of you,
and the day I became a prey,
in your pretty path of life.
How do I call you a fren!
when trust is turned into a tale,
and when friendship is
an etiquette in the end.

The Hint

I weave a dream
of you and me,
hand in hand for all moments,
a smile, a tear together.
Cast out in tides,
waves crashing and receding,
our hearts race and meet
again, and again to heal.
Trapped in time today,
we crawl and cry,
soothing and touching our lives.
A dream awakens
and fills the missing gaps.
The flowers that showered blessings
along the gushes of wind
had given me the hint;
and taught me to believe.

If Only You Seek a Stance

If only you seek a stance;
If only you seek the truth,
It would clear away all doubts,
It would wash open the eyes.
Which way will lead;
Which way? If you lend ears to all,
When your belief is aback,
Wind and will winds and twines up.
Pity pours over your pain,
That you invited unknowingly,
To quarrel and quell yourself,
To sip a borrowed tale.
I only see the variance,
One form taking another.
I fortunately have a stance to seek,
I fortunately have a truth to seek.

Distances Are Lovelier Than Ever

Distances are lovelier than ever,
Distances are better than never.
Smiles bloom
In the rhythm of a lyrical song,
And wishes wreathe your winding paths,
Wishing joy, you ever wish for.
Loneliness was for days bygone,
Lying beside, I am a shadow.
In moments of human folly,
Believing that forgiveness will be mine.
In consciousness, my Lord always be.
In consciousness, my Love always be.

A River That Will Never Stop Flowing

We keep wondering,
what Love is?
It is—
born with us.
It flows uninhibited
in your pure heart.
It teaches,
but we often fail to learn.
It descends,
when we feel—
feel the joy and agony,
together.
It awakens,
our sensibility and ability
to love, love selflessly.
It is,
nourishment of the soul.
It is,
acceptance.

It is,
forgiveness.
Love is,
a river that will never stop flowing.

Don't Wake Me Up

Don't wake me up,
when these sweetest of dreams come.
Don't wake me up,
when this sleep replenishes me.
Don't wake me up,
when the worldly things do not affect me.
Don't wake me up,
when I am in a wonderland.
Don't wake me up,
for these dreams don't come often.
Don't wake me up,
when these sweetest of dreams come.

Let Hearts That Long Meet

Let hearts that long meet,
let nothing come in between.
Let lie belie itself,
let it turn away ashamed.
Let clear light make its way,
to shine bright in our lives.
A few steps taken together shall lead
into a journey of dreams.
The dawn chorus gives company,
as the daunting distance dwindles.
When fearless souls are set to soar,
together against all odds.

My Little One!

My little One!
we had a walk of nine months together,
that only belongs to me and you.
I hated the sight and smell of a grain of food,
and the early months were tiresome months.
There was a sudden shift of moods and
yearnings of sleep.
But you were the hope I was awaiting
and my excitement was elevated,
with your little movements,
and your first kick in my womb.
I wished I could keep you always in my womb,
safe and away from the scary world.
Our walk of nine months is a precious one!
Then our nine months drew closer and closer,
we were both scared of the big moment.
Both of us cried;
your first cry overwhelmed everyone,
and my tears were a happy one.
Your tiny fingers and tiny toes,
your twinkling eyes searching for me,

instantly stole my heart away,
and that very moment;
I found the mother in me,
eager to love you,
My little One!

Sleepless Nights

The day's rush has worn out
the body and mind.
And you, Oh! Sleepless nights—
the hours keep passing,
and these eyes need some rest,
for the day after morn'
is a string of tasks.
Ahh, Sleepless nights!
Steal my unrestful mind,
stop this ticking time,
stop this ticking mind.
Tell me the stories,
in another time.
Tell me the worries,
in another time.
Spare me these sleepless nights,
for these eyes are closed,
these sleeps aren't mine.

SECTION – II

COME CHANGES COME

I'm a Flower Frail

I'm not a maiden fair
        Of a dreamland,
I'm not a fairy
        Of a fairyland.
I'm a servitor sown
        To serve the Almighty;
I'm a humble soul
        To spread His Love.
I'm a flower frail
        Tender to touch,
I'm a beating heart
        Prone to hurt,
I'm a friend's smile
        Ready to share.

The Weak Mind

Weaker and weaker the mind grows,
strength to endure seems lost;
the world goes round and round,
and only differing thoughts rule.
Afraid I am, stronger and bolder to grow;
leaving the path of simplicity,
and meeting the worldly wisdom.
All lies in Thy hands,
He who plays and alters often;
who gives choices hard to choose.
Your test, O Lord! I have failed so far.
Every step I take
takes me farther from myself.
Will I overcome this fight?
the fight of this weakening mind!

Fate and I

Here I am today,
And yesterday is gone.
Tomorrow come what may—
Of transformations galore,
I will be with myself,
Remaining a bit of what I am.
A Fate I cannot change,
The Fate that awaits me!
And so, I walk ahead,
Seeking His Holy Hands.
Nevermore to give up,
With the Lord and His wishes.

Becoming Me

I found myself this day,
after a long, long search;
a wandering me all this while,
and I greet this Grand meeting.
I feel the Birth again,
I glow in the new zeal;
I see my Destiny clear,
blazing my chosen path.
In my efforts, I will endure,
in my dreams, I will believe;
a missing link and I was lost until today,
and binding with it, I begin.
I shall not stop now,
I shall steadily tread my path;
adding to my music strings,
Beads of me, in becoming Me.

I Have Fallen

I have fallen,
fallen from a mountain high.
Floating like a feather-light,
leaving behind all loads,
To land somewhere—
somewhere I never know.
I have no fear,
to break into pieces.
From a scratch,
I shall begin afresh,
and take my time to struggle,
in taking the steps,
to wisdom.
With a hope that keeps me young,
with a smile that cheers me up,
and a tear that gives me strength.
I have fallen and I have no fear;
I float for this moment,
to be back on the track of life.

An Apology

Oh, Almighty! I offer an apology,
Accept earnest atonement to Thee.
No more shall thy child offend,
For days and nights that shall come.
Oh, Moon! An injustice offered to ye,
Let ye be ye and day be day;
Forgive thy child and grant
A favour to laugh and cry.
It is but a fine test of life;
Rise O Bright Sun!
O fragile Moon!
Unhear those prayers,
Bruises and agony;
Not an eternity they are,
A moment of my own pain,
It is to eternity we belong!

A Reason to Live

One life we have,
to create with an Art;
enemies and friends,
reasons only we know.
For we learn sooner or later,
the good are fools,
or truly, are they wise?
Those who deny have a life!
A Life of tests and trials,
and prove to none but to oneself;
to find a light to lead,
to find a reason to live,
A reason—
that keeps the wheels rolling on,
forward,
and remember,
be quiet to be wise.

I Wish to Fly

I wish to fly, fly high,
flying and gliding in the sky;
traversing places new
and yet to return to the nest where I belong.
I wish to stay long
in my mother's abode,
amid immortal love.
I wish traditions were the other way round;
then, I wouldn't have to leave
this paradise that raised me,
where every nook and cranny
is a spring of memory.
I wish life were not different
from years to years;
I wish—
to free myself and unleash
from any compulsion, any oppression,
and fly high.

Come, Changes, Come

Come, changes, come,
come and transform us;
thou cannot limit thy mind,
thy mind, lighter than wind.
Why thou should fear an outcome?
For giving ways to thy tender ideas,
will be more or less a gain.
Abhor surviving in a stagnant pool,
and truly shall thou swell with life;
thou now, who befits a fighter,
a winner of thyself.
Thou do not get startled
even seasons change;
learn, learn vain mind,
these Nature's lessons.

Rest, Rest Unrestful Mind

Rest, rest unrestful mind!
All things are set fine;
you have no race to run,
you have to keep pace of life.
Life may still urge you,
life may still bring worries;
you have to calm the haste,
you have to warm all your worries.
You have enough courage to carry on
and prayers to give you strength.
A work wrapped up is a great boon.
So, rest, rest unrestful mind,
as your duty is done for the day.

A Passing Query

Every day, like a busy bee,
flower to flower, and back to the beehive,
I endeavour to harvest like a bee
and remain engrossed in the day's work.
Sudden but swift, like a gust of wind,
when flashbacks of memories visit,
one by one,
sweet and sour,
making me laugh, making me ponder,
making me lost, lost in a reverie.
Many queries arise,
why, why, why?
Is there still an answer,
and I receive none.
I realise they are just glimpses of the past.
It is beyond, and I find peace again,
and I turn to my duty, my delight!

My Dream

I shall surrender to the stream I fall into—
the stream shall feed me,
water me and refresh me.
I will keep going
with these thoughts;
thoughts of a wanderer, an explorer,
a dreamer, realising its dreams.
Dreams, I will paint with the colours I choose,
and soon I shall be one among them,
carving a special niche.
That's when I shall realise my dream
to throw the world a light
of my living in this world.

Poetry

I find in poetry—
an ecstasy and a wholeness.
As a friend, you hear me out,
and as a deep breath, you calm me down.
Through you,
I believe in the Lord
who blesses, loves me so.
You put life into me,
and free my fire deep,
suggesting me my purpose in life.

The Search

The search in life
begins,
for an untainted space;
where one can breathe
and recline.
The very yearning,
many fear,
yet many aspire.
The search in life unveils
that this untainted space
is all around—
in a string of music,
in a voice that sings and soothes,
in a blank page,
in a truth told,
in the beauty the nature beholds,
and in many countless ways.
Knowing this conflict
of the tainted and untainted
guides us,
in this search of life.

Thing We Believe In

The things we have done have led us
where we stand today,
leaving behind yesterday.
The dreams in the past
are no longer doubts,
but have become a reality.
The mistakes—
big and small we made,
have become the best teachers.
The things we have worked for
have been lost, have been achieved,
shaping our destiny!
The things we dream now—
build a hope
and a goal to work for.
Things we believe in
shall become a reality,
sooner or later, which awaits our arrival!

SECTION – III

HOPE

A Blooming Flower

Flowers are beautiful —sing early birds,
hums buzzing bees,
conveys dancing butterflies,
painting the world in different shades,
spreading beauty of the Divine Creator.
One and all, a uniqueness
in the garden of God;
we are His flowers, we are His colours,
a beauty with a purpose.
Though we never know
when He will pluck us,
how blissful, blessed we would be
plucked by His Holy hands.
And while we bloom,
our simple task lies ahead
to prove our love and worth
with these few more breaths;
before we wither
and enter His Divine Heavenly Abode.

To Time

Time passes, everything passes.
Time changes, things change.
You and I would agree that time decides
and keeps our hopes, our dreams,
memories, faith, and life.
As a temple of test, of trust,
a constant companion, a pendulum swinging back and forth
that brings alive lovely memories,
that builds bonds of the past and the future;
and true to time, standing hills
open green fields witness and await
the travelling Time—
of yore, today, and tomorrow.

Happy a Child Is

Ever thought why a child is happy?
Ever seen a child play tirelessly?
Ever seen a child smile with all its heart?
Ever seen a child cry all out of rhyme?
All that springs is love,
all that springs is trust;
no worldly gains in mind
and no worries for an end.
Cheers and laughter,
ever asking and ever learning;
their innocence and rich heart
emerge in their eyes and sparkle.
Ever tried to understand them?
No friend! You need not understand them.
All you need is to love them,
happy that a child is and will be.

Life

Life is verily a dream,
a journey of wildest imaginings,
with an unfailing end
and so many things to do.
The rein is in our fists
to venture into the unknown,
yielding all apprehensions to the Almighty.
To reap newness and happiness,
and the present moment is the greatest gift;
a possibility to fulfil our dreams.

Dreams

Dreams—
A secret, sacred, and sole world for me
and for all to be in a fantasy.
What do we not see in dreams?
Our nearest and dearest folks,
known and unknown places,
flashing, connecting, revealing hidden hopes,
taking us on a roller coaster ride.
And sometimes in the form of a messenger, a foresight—
empowering us to foresee,
things that happen without fail.
Formless and intangible you are, O! Dreams,
beyond words, beyond time and space.
Privileged I am to see one more time
my beloved ones which I will never see in this world,
truly a mystery you will be;
unwarned, uninvited you come and
leave memories lingering in our minds.

Hope

When the world is a whirlwind
and you are at a standstill,
we often slip into a temptation
to the sunken depths of a falling;
a pull of becoming one with darkness,
and you are one with your shadow.
Screams and whistles are unheard then,
the crowd keeps moving steadily,
and you own a struggling space alone,
far away from the noises and people.
You lean back, look beyond and behold;
you search and feel it deep,
a peace profound, untouched within.
Like a light at the end of the tunnel,
hope holds out to help and lead us on,
Hope is what we often call Life,
soft and tender yet strong and promising.
Life is, as long as hope is.

My Motherland, My Precious

The grasses green are glowing,
the sun bright is warming,
the blue sky is spreading,
the chirpy birds are singing.
My Motherland, my precious!
Her flawless enchantment,
her glittering rivers,
meandering hills after hills.
Butterflies are dancing in pairs,
the red blooms peacefully among the green.
Honking vehicles break this tuning;
bringing chatters of what is happening—
My Motherland, my precious!
Is in distress,
tough times that trailed
have stayed and not gone.
Wiser, they say, to leave,
better a place and people to see,
but true daughters and sons
do stay and do return.
To heal our Mother's wound,

to answer the call of duty,
for every land has a story
of struggle long and ultimate victory.
As brothers and sisters, we dwell
in the hills and in a vale,
under a roof of love and beauty,
under her nature pristine.
Why then do we turn to—
ways of intolerance!
In hours when our Mother needs us,
in hours of her agony.
Wiser, are they?
To leave her in pain
and abandon her for a better place
where every need seems fulfilled.
My Motherland, my precious!
Is caught in a web.
My Mother, your peace
will return in the days to come.

With hope, you persist—
with hope, you always fought.
Your resilience
will lead us through.

My Motherland, my precious!
You will flourish far and wide.
Unsung, your beauty will be heard
when the blood of sons will mix as one.

Thy Hatred

In silence, my tears yell
when I face up to hatred;
harsh is thy hatred's nature,
in words, in thoughts, in deeds.
Bounded in greed
where one lives in fear and anger
and lone progress;
why choose such a life
which dampens the spirits of others?
A time will come
when hearts will bleed in tears,
with moments unbearable
if hatred veils our lives.
I would rather choose
peace, at least humility,
dignity, respect, and honour.
Where laughter meets
and open hearts rejoice
its victory over hatred!

Winter Days

Winter days, we used to long for you.
When you came, came our free days,
and we played with full zest,
with full right and might.
Morning to noon, noon to night—
and we crawled back into the warmth,
the warmth of the hearth,
with stories galore to hear,
that stretched our imaginations,
and those were the lovely days.
Winter days, winter days!
These days you bring no free days.
Pale is the colour of our faces,
duty-laden and thoughts-laden,
in a fancy world
where we are caught up in the show
to earn the laugh and applause
of all the intent spectators.

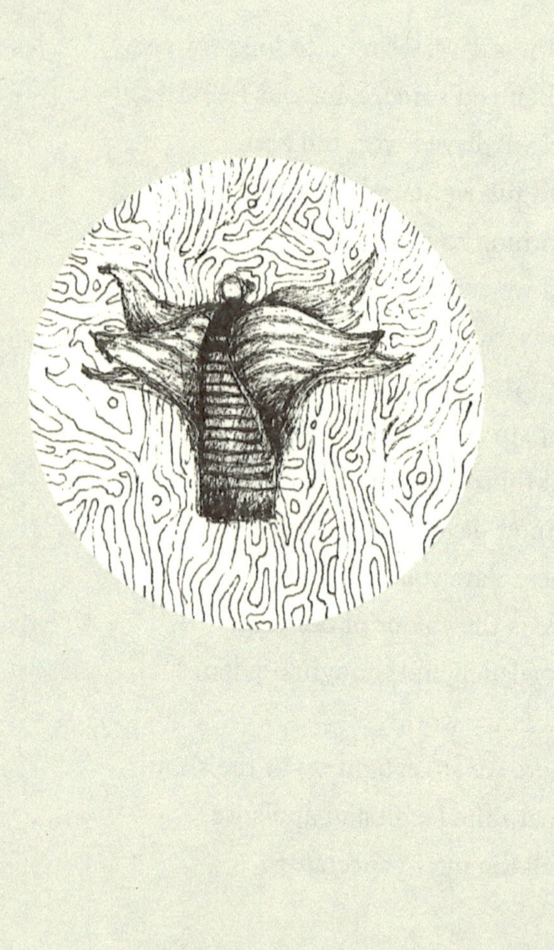

She

She is a woman.
The day she is born;
her parents feel the burden
for she is only a guest,
a guest in the house—
until she gets married.
She is a woman.
Of dreams and aspirations,
Oh! What a silly thought.
Go, go and wash the clothes for your brothers,
go, go and make some tea for the family,
go, go and learn to cook food, and finish your chores.
She is a woman.
Start searching for your other half,
the better half?
Find your destiny,
find your home.
She is torn, torn apart.

She is a woman.
She seeks talent, not a better half,

she seeks love, not a shelter,
she seeks life, not destiny,
and she is not a burden
to be thrown and disowned.
She is a woman.
She has to survive;
no matter what.
She is the change
that you have to accept.
She will live and lead.
She is a woman.
How long will it take?
To treat her as an equal,
to give her the same rights,
to let her feel the way she feels,
and let her be the way she wants.
She is a woman.
She is not a shadow.
Life is where she is.
She is the mother of life!
Treat her with respect,
not as a pleasure and a desire.
She is a woman.
She is not a burden.
The very thought of it is a burden!

That generations have preached,
generations who treated her unfairly.
It is time to eradicate this very thought.
She is a woman.
It is not her privilege
to take care of the world around her.
Give her freedom.
Do not enslave her
in her family, in all walks of life.
She is a woman.
Her birth is a celebration;
as much as the celebration of his birth.
Every lesson taught to her
should be taught to him.
And every lesson taught to him
should be taught to her.

Sharing Your Dilemma

In this mundane existence,
Oh! My dear friends,
Oh! Don't get lost in it,
don't get lost in a dilemma!
Wait awhile, take your time
to ask who we are and why were we born.
Aren't we a soul, fully awake and active,
a soul that smiles and shares,
ever ready to devote to our assigned tasks,
ever ready to devote to our fellow beings?
Life is large, expanding beyond you and me.
Life is to rejoice in service to all.
Life is to surrender unto the Lord!

My Prayer to Thee

At every dawn, my prayer to Thee—
awake this soul with thy melodies,
Shine thy morning rays
showing the path of truth.
Bless this soul a bright day,
and with Thy guidance,
I shall walk without fear and worry
in doing a rightful deed.
Thou manifest in myriad miracles
and heal all wounds.
At every night, my prayer to Thee
is to thank Thee for everything.

Friendship

Travelling in this vast, unending sea,
will, courage, faith come to the calling;
with strength, we may swim across the sea,
but as the sun fades, a stormy night arrives.
Sailing, a ship comes to our rescue
and takes us on board,
Friendship sails us through the rippling waves
in the sparkling blue;
sharing a space to stay and survive.
Hail up such a journey—
a journey with your friends!
With trust, love, help, and sacrifice;
cheers, cheers to all
to those who board Friendship in life.

Beauty It Is

I walk past and see my reflection in the serene lake,
I stay and stare for long;
Is it my image, is it a mirage?
I throw a stone to see.
Gently it waves away the stillness,
telling me it isn't a mirage;
the ripples recede
and the calmness returns.
A raindrop falls to break her calmness again,
No! not to send ripples;
it has come, come to join her
to make her alive.
Drops and drops join and fall,
pouring, dancing joyfully with her;
all the reflections gone,
all the mirages gone.
There's none so valuable,
there's none so beautiful
than the truth descending on our hearts.

Revelation of Thy Presence

Life has unveiled Thy presence,
the secrecy and mystery
of the Ultimate, the Absolute truth
of His Divine Grace,
of His wishes and plays;
mirthful, peaceful, and blissful
of the Almighty Supreme Lord!
As a child,
Thy eternity I wondered,
enlightened I am today
of the eternal soul;
that yearns to offer
a devotion—
to the Supreme Lord
by way of service to mankind,
in their hours of need.
I walk in Thy light
to service and liberation.

A Walk in Unity

Sisters and brothers,
ripe is this time right is this moment;
to release us from bondage,
to rebuild our Motherland.
Laughter in our valley
echoed in our hills too.
O! Why do we fight?
A Destiny common we have to reach,
to relive the liveliness
of beauty and peace, we had!
Of the love and trust of sisters and brothers—
in pieces, we can never be
as we dwell in one soul of our Motherland.
Why are we trying to tear ourselves apart?
Let us now abide by and merge
against all forces that pull us apart.
Hand in hand, let us rise,
let us take a step forward,
and begin a walk, in unity,
never to stop until our Destiny is reached.

A Reinvention

Is life a sheer subsistence?
Or a figment, a fallacy,
or is life a vision?
Or an unending, incessant narrative,
a story within a story;
so much to fathom.
Life is a seed to sow—
to unearth and lure richness.
O! Mighty ideas, of one's intuition, sensibilities;
life is but a Reinvention.

Nature Quiet Nature

Music flows around in nature;
in tunes comes the music.
In murmurs and in silence,
in darkness and in lone rumination,
Nature, quiet nature plays the music.
When one delves in contemplation;
one finds joy and sorrow in unison,
one becomes love and hatred.
Nature, quiet nature preserves a sanctity;
where we can rest and feel the tranquillity.
The infinite blue sky tells us to expand beyond;
the white clouds tell us to drift away and to travel.
The gurgling river tells us to be cheerful,
the mighty mountains tell us to be resilient.
Nature teaches us to heal;
and bestows us with an inspiration
to perceive and to learn the ways of
Nature, quiet nature.

Thy Humbleness

Thankfulness, a fragrance is in the air,
not in words, not in measure
is thy humbleness.
No requital, no bargaining
to travel this far,
to travel further the road.
To stand up
against any tide,
thy humbleness
is a healing balm.
How many ways there exist
For harmony to persist?
the only way—
alone is thy humbleness.

Equality

Charity begins at home!
Yes, we all agree.
Equality begins at home!
Do we all agree?
A girl is taught to care about every nook and corner of the home;
she is taught to clean and to cook.
A boy is taught to explore what he wants;
he is taught to wash his hands, eat, and to take rest.
Oh! Is it equality then?
She is taught to serve and he is taught to be served.
Equality begins at home.
Do we all agree then?
Charity begins at home.
Let equality begin at home!

Midnight

In the midst of the night,
in the midst of the dark sky.
No one knows what the other feels,
whether the twinkling stars smile,
whether the twinkling star cries.
In the midst of the night,
when the mind wanders,
beyond barriers.
No one knows what the other feels,
and no one knows what the other thinks.
When the night descends,
the darkness shrouds,
and everyone takes refuge
to set the self free—
free of judgements, free of prejudice,
free of burdened hearts and heads,
to embrace the free soul for a peaceful sleep.

In This Path of Life

The rush and crowd in worship;
of the chime, the chanting and the offerings.
To invoke and gather blessings,
all seems to fall,
fall into their proper place of chaos.
A chase of our own shadow
for peace and power dwells within
in solitude and contemplation,
whence truth transpires and illuminates
a path with no trail of fear,
where ideas and hopes spring.
If only we seek this clarity!
If only we break down the barriers and fences,
and the volcano of hatred embedded—
may it be flooded by love and compassion!
If only we learn to
discern anger that destroys, love that always builds.
If only we look at the fair reflection
in the mirror of life that never fails,
showing that a destiny lies in our hands;

ploughing and sowing
the seeds of a strong will.
If only we learn to rejoice in failure as a giving of no-return
as much as we celebrate victory;
If only we blend in both heart and mind
with a heart devoid of vices and
a mind tamed upright in control of life;
in this path of life—
let every moment kindle a hope,
a new inspiration and a new beginning.

About the Author

Sonia Oinam was born in Imphal, Manipur, India. As a young girl, she had started writing poetry during her school days. She continued writing articles, letter to the editors, poems in local newspapers during her graduation and post-graduation days. She completed her B.Sc. Zoology (Hons) from Ghanapriya Women's College, and Masters in Life Sciences and Ph.D. from Manipur University. She joined Manipur Civil Service in 2012 and is presently serving as Joint Secretary to Government of Manipur. The first book she completed was her Doctoral thesis 'Nematode Fauna of Cold Blooded Vertebrates of Manipur'.

Sonia always had a fascination with writing and has a keen interest in writing articles, poetry and memoirs. She loves travelling and exploring different places, people, culture, flora and fauna around the world.

www.ingramcontent.com/pod-product-compliance
Lightning Source LLC
LaVergne TN
LVHW091049150826
845673LV00002B/522

* 9 7 9 8 8 9 1 8 6 5 5 6 3 *